Sizzle, Soar, Glow, Roar

Earth Pulse Arias

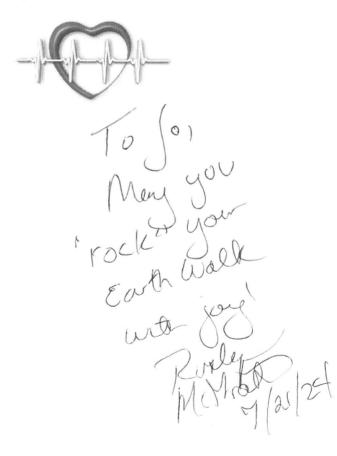

To Jo,
Meny you
'rock' your
Earth Walk
with joy!
Rixley
McMhall
7/25/24

Also by Roslyn Elena McGrath

*Goddess Heart Dancing: A Self-Gided Pathway to Light
through Imagery, Insights & Inspiration*
Volume II of the Goddess Wisdom series

*Goddess Heart Rising
Paintings, Poems & Meditations for Activating Your Divine
Potential* Volume I of the *Goddess Wisdom* series

Post-Resurrection: The Family of Mary Magdalene

*The Third Mary: 55 Messages
for Empowering Truth, Peace & Grace
from the Mother of Mary Magdalene*

*Creative Wisdom Emerging
11 Steps to Advanced Use of Your Creative Wisdom Cards*

*Creative Wisdom Cards & Meditations
for Personal Growth*

*Chakras Alive!
Exploring & Expanding Your Inner Rainbow*

*A New Radiance:
Chakra Blessings from the Divine Feminine
Meditation CD*

SIZZLE, SOAR, GLOW, ROAR
Earth Pulse Arias

Volume I of The Light Dance Spelunking Series

Roslyn Elena McGrath

Chrysaetos Press

Published by Chrysaetos Press 🦅

Contact the publisher for book sales at:

Info@EmpoweringLightworks.com
www.EmpoweringLightworks.com

Printed in the U.S.A.

ISBN-13: 978-0-578-86025-1

To all the elements that love us into being.

Table of Contents

Creation's Orchestra

If I were an instrument,

would I ripple my well-tuned ivories?

Da-da-daah bass drum beats?

Wail through brassy curved funnels?

If I were an instrument,

would I shimmer my round, curved metal?

Submerge in orchestral seas?

Trumpet solo?

Magnify quartets?

If I were an instrument,

would I sing one note long enough to hear it clearly,

send it spinning over ice bridges and melted valleys

to echo through transcontinental treetops?

Dazzle arpeggios with new riffs?

Claim the sound of cold dawn on a mountain top?

*   *   *

Birds warble a weave of simultaneity,

calibrating our chaos into calm.

Ocean beats massage boulders into pebbles

into beaches of shining color-sounds.

Winds blow leaves and hats and harpsichords into harmony.

Fire crackles old forms, burning their weight down to rising clouds,

lifting their haze through blazing freedom.

Hearts hammer chambers into reworked cavities,

pouring supplies through winding streams of all bodies,

all blood-borne instruments of life.

We pulse with an ongoing orchestra reverberating

through our world.

Dream Life

Listen to the language of pressurized life

within the heft of rock and stone.

It will lead you into earth

and eventually to wide, wide sea,

where blue-green waves strike shore,

shaping sediment as I awaken

into the pulse beat of my Mother Earth

who sings unceasingly as waves smack land,

and gulls shriek over and over again.

Fission and fusion spark elements into existence

through broiling stars who sing their song

to the blue-green rock I call home

as I pass through streams of Light and Sound

on my inward orbit,

soaking in sensation after sensation-

a dream, a life, a dream.

Arose

Once upon a time in the Land of the Divine,

grew a very old plant,

weighty with hundreds of full-headed roses,

fed by hardy soils, rays of a star, and rainbow raindrops.

One day, a small honeybee buzzed into the center of the largest rose

whose glorious scent inspired deep-breathing smiles throughout the land.

The bee was enchanted by the thought of the nectar

 within such a universe of velvet-silk and bursting pollen.

And the rose embraced this small bee as none other,

drinking in its busyness as cherishment in action,

a dance of adoring that fulfilled the rose's purpose

of nourishing beauty—a soul contract in action.

When the bee was heavy with all the pollen it could carry,

it rose in ecstasy, hovered in thanks,

and flew off to share the jewels of its experience.

And the rose exulted into even greater openness,

'til its center became a doorway,

and each petal began to share itself uniquely,

floating off unbound.

I popped my head inside this portal

and have never been the same.

Winded

She was woken by wind,

its plaintive gusts resounding through eaves

and battering windows.

She was lifted up by wind,

held suspended over twisted bed sheets

in her horizontal, at-rest position.

She was penetrated by wind,

its wildness entering and loosening

the spaces between each cell.

She was sucked out into night by wind,

through an unexpected opening

in her bedroom wall.

She was carried off by wind,

its currents dispersing pieces of her in every direction,

spreading her thinly, hugely,

and nearly undetectably

throughout the planet, stars, galaxy....

She was motivated by wind,

lifting as it lifted, soaring as it soared,

crashing as it crashed.

She was educated by wind,

touching what it touched,

finding what it found.

She was swept back toward herself by wind,

as it brushed her particles

into a shimmering, vibrating pile.

She was reunited by wind,

each aspect of her newfound being

swirled into stronger connection with all the others.

She was revealed to herself by wind,

as it tumbled over new contours

and hushed against soft edges.

She understood herself through wind,

mimicking its patterns, bending with its currents,

and listening to its ancient, changing voice.

She was brought back to herself by wind,

rolling inward with its wake and touching spaces

within spaces within spaces within herself.

She was made whole by wind,

as it stirred inner with outer,

spinning all together in a blend beyond imagining.

She was poured out by wind,

adding more glimmer to star shine and dewdrops,

more lilt to its song.

Internal Medicine
(Medicine Song for Genean Granger)

Heart, lungs,

heart, lungs,

beating out a song,

breathing to fuel

your life

this minute.

Hurry now, notice

that you're living in it!

Heart, lungs,

lungs, heart,

breathe it in, now that's a start!

Sing out

your taut drum.

Notice what your songs become.

Breathe out,

breathe in,

welcome to

the thoughts that spin,

making circles in your head,

filling out across your bed.

Lungs, heart,

heart, lungs,

breathe into

the now that's sprung

from the warm beat

of your strong heart.

Live to this music

that's powered your start.

Breathe out,

breathe in,

each new moment

is a moment to grin.

Breathe in,

breathe out.

Trust in the future

that's waiting to spout.

Breathe out,

breathe in.

You live to the pump

that lures you within.

Breathe in,

breathe out,

your joy thumps in beauty

lustrous inside and out.

Heart, lungs,

lungs, heart,

your gems of creating

circle 'round the living art

of your breathing in

and your breathing out.

Just to be here, truly be here,

that's what Life is all about.

Oceans of Forests

Oceans of forests

wave brilliant green tops

'gainst azure-laid sunsets

and spongy cloud mops.

They breathe for the planet.

They shelter the earth.

They anchor the granules

of moistly rich dirt.

They listen for openings

in our minds and our hearts,

to usher in new leaves

to grow us fresh thoughts

that dance through the air,

uplifted by wind.

They sing songs together,

blow us new rhythms.

The thoughts of the forest

refresh from on high,

tingling our goose flesh

with a glimmer and sigh.

Anniversary

My bones arose from salty sea,

melding marine life into marrow.

They drew blood from stones

and skin from fragments of fallen harvests,

sculpted organs from rumble of ocean wave,

gull squawk, herons' flight,

built muscle out of earthen animal homes,

and cartilage from sea foam.

They married marvels of chlorophyll,

star shine, and silica

to materialize soul through irises,

ear-ises, and orifices.

These gifts from my mother

gush golden abundance

unsheltered by timefulness

in this organ recital

on the sacred anniversary of our death.

What the Dolphins Told Me Long Ago

Waves of water

rush through

our playing field,

divine in their method of motion.

The stir of the Ocean

is a fabulous song.

It stirs our hearts

and makes us long

for the star-filled nights

that adjust our sails,

lighten our loads,

and strengthen our tails.

We love to visit the beautiful skies,

our fellow swimmers,

and the tides that glide.

We trinkle tranquil through the course

of the underwater seaview

and the rocking seahorse.

We understand the Love that guides

each part of the All,

each ripple of this ride.

We share our knowing with all we see.

Our cosmic glowing is wrinkly

with the lines of Divinity –

Our sonar range is growing,

and the power of this aspect

lies in setting free our knowing

with our backsplash and our tails,

our leaping together and our wails

of tolerance and trust,

our mutuality-must.

It's a game of inner knowing.

as we scribe our hearts are showing

that the saturated glowing

of our skins are naught

but a trace of all that's depicted

through our elemental knot

of earth and sun and sky,

of water, wind, and why,

as the lengthened days go by,

enumerating our love

for all below, and all above.

Do you see us as we am now?

Do you see us as we are?

Have we got the "gitchee-gumee"

that will elevate our star

from its hidden-by-delusion,

from its hidden-by-the-scars

of the lovers of Illusion,

of the Wrinkle-Master's cards?

It's a game now, we are playing

with our eloquent delight

for we love to smack you silly

with our treatises so bright!

We're aware of all your folly,

but we're ever raptured more

by the way you can be jolly

and your opening of the door

to opportunity for true immunity

from cradle-robbing things,

and your exploration/maturation

of coward-canceling wings!

For we will find you and sit behind you

when you care to cooperate here.

We will find you and sit behind you

helping your mind to clear

and set its path free from Illusion,

drawing the All-One conclusion

that All is possible here!

So take care!

Don't swear,

but live your life as you please.

Take a drive with our thoughts to wive

and happenstance will make clear

that we hold you all very dear.

So look to us as your mirror

and find all of Life getting clearer!

Take care!

Don't swear!

Enjoy, En-Joy,

En-Dear!!!!!

Heating Up

Unbridled matches

weave blinding-hot tongues

through dry-kindled leaves

and thoughts now unsprung.

They ripple 'round corners,

flambé-ing each road,

melting the stop signs

and crackling in code.

They singe roofs and porches.

They fire up the town.

They motivate red wagons

to hastily gather 'round.

They cannot be outed.

They hunger for more

to pillage and crumble

old over-ripe stores.

They heat up the garden.

They melt down the hose.

They steam through the orchards.

They cannot be thrown

from their mission of fission

to rework the world,

to kindle the concepts

that make good this purge.

They devour stray cacti.

They continue their hiss.

They'll rival the sun's shine

'til all melds to bliss.

At Heart

I long to reach inside my heart

and grab a little piece

to remind me of its beauty,

its pink pulsing strength,

its dependable central core

of my beating, breathing life.

I long to move deeper inside my heart

to marvel at four linked chambers

pouring out blue-blood troops

while receiving their journey-tarnished brethren

back for cleansing and renewal.

What stories would these platelets and their comrades tell

of their twenty-thousand-league passage

through veins, arteries, arterioles, capillaries,

feeding masses of muscle, organ, and tissue,

of the epics of obstacles they'd swum over, around, and through,

surging with the changing-tempo current

of their million-miled lives.

Love Note to Summer

I take my clothes off to you.

You heat me up and leave me thirsting for more.

You ripen, then electrify me

with your thunder and lightning,

melt me with myriad blossoms and birdsongs,

feed me your fresh produce,

soak me in your long glowing light.

Crickets and frogs croak lullabies in scant-sleep nights

while bonfires sizzle before early dawn.

Though your embrace can exhaust me,

I would wear it forever.

But that is not your nature.

And so, I keep your fire burning

in my being through the seasons

until you return.

Awakening

I woke up knowing
the day was special.
Air glowed fresh, wind-cleared,
radiant with opportunity.

Then the Thought Thief came,
clearing me out of lofty goals,
and I sat dumb, breathless,
with nothing to think,
seeing only color and shape,
no objects,
hearing only sounds, no stories,
words, or activities.
Flung into a world
stripped of interpretation,
what illusion could save me now?

In another time,
sweet peace delivered itself through the trees
as a breeze curling 'round my skin.
When I shut my eyes,
fairy lilies danced in tune with the weather.

I always thought the trees were speaking to me,
waving their limbs as our car strode by on the highway,

welcoming me, and inviting me to stay much longer.

I imagined myself living there in the woods,

without thought or need for fuel,

electricity or refrigeration.

Everything was just there for the taking, for appreciating.

I'm certain the fairies enjoyed my company then,

though I had no conscious awareness of them.

And when I sang myself to sleep at night,

chances are they joined in.

Still, Pearl of the Sky glimmers

between clouds, gazing down

on sleeper and sleepless alike. Her soft, cool

whisper shifts their night-glazed forms

into poetic majesty,

as she lights them in unusual places.

Earth Meal

Food is meant to be eaten on skin,

not metal, nor wood.

"You leave that dirt alone,"

says the man on my left to his child.

But what if that dirt is richer

than anything you've ever tasted?

What if the soil, run deep with roots,

is filled with calcium and iron beyond your imagining,

and California raisins were discovered inside them?

I wonder if anyone's ever tried

to improve upon this flavor,

or if they've just let it be.

Imagine it toasted with chocolate sauce,

or ground into a fine consistency,

then spread with bananas and nuts.

Whole grain might be tasty too.

If you were to go hungry, for just one day,

would you sample some and recognize this harvest?

I came that way,

a dirt-digging, worm-eating,

Mother Earth-swallowing fool.

And I'll remain that way

'til the end of my days.

Potato

Thin skin covers yellow, meaty flesh,

mined from the dark,

trucked to stands and stores,

exchanged for coins and papers,

and delivered to homes

where they are softened and sweetened

by heat and moisture,

punctured by metallic blades and tines,

consumed by gnashing molars, sweeping tongue,

tunnel of throat, and bobbing Adam's apple

into the fires and streams of your alimentary system,

burgeoning nutrients and wastes

winding through new territories

back to loam.

Leaving

They turn to flame, puce, gold, vermilion,

lighting up the skies with their extravagance.

They release the ties through which they've been bound,

then waft, whip, eddy down

to pavement, soil, gutters, rooftops,

are strenuously gathered into masses

along curbs and street corners

until marshalled by wind to migrate

past roads, yards, fences,

spread into new configurations.

Some will be retrieved to their former piles by harried humans,

others will be abandoned to Nature's notions,

unintendedly mulching corners of yards,

growing slimy beneath snow,

gradually giving up their veined structures

to feed the dirt and its denizens.

Ancient Wind

Day upon day, the ceaseless moan continued,

reverberating through housetops,

horse ranches, bedside manors,

sweeping through doors, ear drums,

phones, and phonetics.

It rumbled through windows, doorways,

small bowling alleys, and pizza parlors,

past mansions, skyscrapers, billboards, factories.

It carried peanuts, pocketbooks,

household receipts, laughter,

lilies, and song sheets.

It roared into basements, hideaways,

hilltops, and locked doors,

vibrating menus, mealtimes, and missing persons.

Its stops are ominous with suspense,

for it can reawaken with a crack,

tearing sidewalks,

ripping branches,

catapulting consciousness with its ancient howl

for it began before humans begot,

before trees were strong and grass had grown,

and it will continue long after

a world we know has gone.

Winter Moon Madness

Winter moon madness sparkles sharply

over crusty layers of icy skyfall.

It ripples through frigid rivers,

captures cold shadows,

deepens their inky contrast

to the shining white

that blurs shapes and freezes forms.

Can color continue in this world?

Must all be shades of dark and light,

ad nauseum, forever?

When the moon conquers our souls,

will we remain frozen,

caught up in mental maneuvers,

statues under indigo skies?

Or will we reach out,

grab another's hand,

and dance wildly to the sound

of our own howling laughter,

kissing shadows and sparkles

'til we keel over

drunk with frosted breath?

Softened World

Frozen quiet

whips the sound

of two hearts clacking

into silence

where they find white cold horizons

waiting for shrieking

north wind's blast.

Ancient stronghold

of hidden talents

sits below frosted gardens,

clasping these treasures

'til pale sun deepens warm,

persuading spaces to open, allow,

engage gently with a softened world.

Melt Down

My world has gone marshmallow

with white piles poured over

straight lines and rigid forms

of roads and cars and homes –

a place for crisp shadows

of the few verticals tall enough to rise through them,

past their rounded similarizing

of all that lies below.

They have melted down my method of navigating,

blending plans and purposes with vivid white dreams

and curling-in compromises, countering calls to action

with whiffs of fragrant fats, sweet meats.

Ice shards radiate the colors

of their next-of-kin,

stabbing soft snow,

punctuating changing skies.

I live for the day of their demise

into streaming pools that open the ground

to drink in the sky effortlessly once again,

and reveal all that was frozen beneath.

Beneath Winter

Beneath snow, below cement,

beyond topsoil, under roots,

down past spring and geological strata,

is the beating furnace,

the boiling bristle

of Mother Earth's heart,

feeding magma to all She creates.

The mystery of Her rising

steams the air,

pollinates the flora,

gives minerals to blood and bone

and hoof and wing,

supports the treasures She lays bare

to the long rays of Father Sun.

Sea Sound

Now Moment

Breath, Pray.

Light on water,

Light of day.

Gifts of being,

Seeing, Do

create your play time.

See anew.

Pens are scratching.

Writing elves

sit on couches,

chairs, and shelves.

Winter's warming.

Lunch, the next course

Fuel is heated,

warmth from the source.

Play it lightly,

play it well.

All the world's

your tale to tell.

Sing it softly,

sing it loud.

Sway with purpose.

Show you're proud

of living fully,

of living free,

of charting your course

so effortlessly.

The sands of time

have swum away,

and all the oceans

rise up to say,

Swoosh.

Roll.

Rustle.

Swell.

Sweep closely in,

away as well.

Ebb.

Whisper.

Roar.

Sh-shine.

Keep your reflections

changing, like mine.

Hum.

Soothe.

Sound.

Fish.

Cast in your treasure.

Marry your bliss.

Sleep soundly

in our lullaby.

Whistle your romance.

Carry on with your high

that rolls, swells,

ebbs, sways.

These are the true times,

these are the days

of following through

on your soul's hush.

It elevates your goals.

It signals your rush

into high waters

that sweep you to the west,

and support you all your days.

Sing song,

hints of hunts

through pearly-green waters

and elemental punts

of green-gray-violet light

that shimmers over edges,

that shimmers over fronts

of cottages and cabins,

of tree trunks and doors,

of ever-fruitful harvests,

of ever-fruitful moors,

where silence sings

to the full moon,

and waves grab ahold

of its rising tune,

as we sing songs

that shell the night

into pearls of wisdom,

into pearls of delight.

Equinotic Bliss

Mountain gorge song
cascaded down through crystallized trees
into secret waters below,
shattering their stillness.

It echoed 'cross brilliant skies,
bounded through billowing clouds,
and landed lightly on the beak
of the first robin.

I wandered out of my home,
bedazzled by white walls withering
into small lakes on my front yard,
inhaled the echo of spring's thaw,
breathed cool light
into small spaces between my pores,
thrusted outstretched arms
into newly tunneled time,
tipped into equinotic bliss.

A River Runs Through Us

A river runs through us,

winding corpuscles and minerals to their destinies,

sweeping bile and salt waters through ducts,

surging saliva, semen, and womb wellings

with desire-driven alacrity,

spewing waste-water out our bottoms,

diamond drops out our eyes,

dew from our pores,

aromas from our innards.

We are born from waters

and some say we evolved from the sea.

Algae still clings to some of us.

And while we are tossed by storms,

we cannot survive without wetness within and without.

Our internal climate cannot take the heat

of our alchemical processes,

the weight of our bones,

the friction of our contractions and expansions,

the electricity of our synapses,

without the lubricant of fluidity,

the streams of nutrient transport,

the flow of worlds-within-worlds

as they pour from, into, and between

us, frogs, trees, clouds,

water tables, lakes, and oceans

of slippery, wild, wet.

First Day Out

Something woke me.

I cannot say what,

even though I didn't know I'd been sleeping.

My shell rubbed more and more tightly

against my soft innards

'til finally the top cracked open

and I expanded up toward the unknown.

Sticky loam and scratchy pebbles

surrounded my pale, fleshy stretch,

'til I emerged into the blue.

The Light was unstoppable,

as was my itch to move toward its source.

I grew greener, taller, stronger.

I leafed to the left and the right.

I opened more of me than I knew existed,

so I could breathe more Light,

lay my burgeoning white silk

on ephemeral azure.

More life stirred and shifted around me,

following its urge to receive, to grow,

to bare itself to the wonders

of our first day out.

Revolution

Hard-packed ground

and frozen white cracked

open in the Light which beckoned

snowdrops, cattails, bird song,

chipmunk blink, squirrel chatter,

flushed ponds with formerly-frozen gushes of fluid,

condensed the dark to shorter frolics,

found pale skins unfettered from layers

of wool, and down, and leather,

revealed new moments as it spun

through the deep, birthing worlds

with its revolution.

Incarnate

Birthing through the Cosmos,

beyond the speed of light,

your trail of stardust spirals

elements, makes possible your life.

The dance continues growing

as more facets do cohere,

refining their relationships,

and particularizing their spheres.

The essence of your nature

speaks to all the parts,

aligning them with your purpose,

and lighting them up with your spark.

To all of this is added

a special umbilical cord

that functions as a ladder

to your Source/Creator/Lord.

When all the mix is established,

your angels waft therein,

adding more light and softness

to the journey you'll begin.

Their shimmers send re-membrance

of God's essential light

to wake you up at crossroads
where darkness dims your sight.

The reasons you incarnate
and the reasons that you fear
are all aligned to make up
a depth of traveling clear.
Through epics you will wander
inviting quandaries to appear.
They'll thicken in your stew-pot,
gradually nourish your sphere.

The lessons that you master
are of the curriculum you've made
to expand the reach of Godness
and the possibilities It creates.

Whenever you are lonesome,
reach within to touch your Light.
It expands your true awareness
of the tribe that knows your might,
and opens your mind to the beauties
offered to you within Life.

We *all* are part of the windfall
that Life-Force Creator has called
in an ever-evolving Universe
of plentifulness installed.

Acknowledgments

This life, these thoughts, this book, its paper, my breath would not be without the body and being of Earth, and the inspiration of Creation.

My heart is full of gratitude for my Writing Group's twenty-plus years' cradle of time, space, and support. within which most of these writings were first formed, and for the examples and encouragement of its members—Christine Saari, Genean Granger, Kristine Granger, Stella Hansen, Maria Formolo, and founder Helen Haskell Remien, for the creative prompts, poetry exposure and encouragement of two-time U.P. poet laureate Martin Achatz's workshops, in which the additional poems here were conceived, for Janeen Pergrin Rastall and Maria Formolo's invaluable, incisive, and encouraging editing support, the early nature time provided by my parents' appreciation, my mother Alma and dear friend Joy Regina Melchezidek's encouragement, my husband Kevin's appreciation, our cockapoo Iggy's boundless love, and the knowing hand of all that guides me.

About the Author

 Roslyn Elena McGrath delights in the magic of nature, and the magic in the nature of Earth's minerals, plants, and animals, including humans. She facilitates healing arts workshops, webinars, and private sessions for self-actualization nationwide and internationallly. She is also the author of *Goddess Heart Dancing: A Self-Guided Pathway to Light; Goddess Heart Rising: Paintings, Poems & Meditations for Activating Your Divine Potential; Chakras Alive! Exploring & Expanding Your Inner Rainbow; Post-Resurrection: The Family of Mary Magdalene; The Third Mary: 55 Messages for Empowering Truth, Peace & Grace from the Mother of Mary Magdalene; Creative Wisdom Emerging: 11 Steps to Advanced Use of Your Creative Wisdom Cards;* and is the author, illustrator, and narrator of *Creative Wisdom Cards & Meditations.*

You can find out more about Roslyn Elena McGrath's books, services, and other creations at www.EmpoweringLightworks.com, and follow her on Facebook at Empowering Lightworks.

More from Roslyn Elena McGrath

Creative Wisdom Cards for Personal Growth - 33 cards with vibrant images drawn from the spiritual level of Nature, and gentle clear wisdom on the back, plus a purple velvet pouch for safekeeping.

Both the imagery and written insights are specially designed to help you:

- Discover new freedom-creating perspectives on old challenges
- Better recognize and act upon your true needs and desires
- Share more compassion with yourself and others
- Experience your interconnection with All Life
- More fully experience our oneness, wholeness and infinite possibilities

Creative Wisdom Meditations - 6 soothing, uplifting meditations inspired by *Creative Wisdom Cards* to help you with the main challenges of life: Self-Nurturance; Acceptance & Confidence in the Cycles of Life; Self-Empowerment; Seeding Your Dreams Into Existence; Shifting Perspective; and Oneness with All-That-Is.

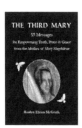

Post-Resurrection: The Family of Mary Magdalene - Discover secrets of our past, present, and future through a new vision of the Holy Family. A story of love, devotion to spiritual evolution, and wisdom for the ages is shared through the messages channeled from Mary Magdalene, Jesus of Nazareth, their spiritually-conceived children, her sister Martha, and Judas Iscariot in this powerful follow-up to *The Third Mary: Messages for Empowering Truth, Peace & Grace from the Mother of Mary Magdalene.* You'll discover their personal struggles, gifts, and lessons learned, witness their spiritual growth and teachings, and absorb their individual forms of support and advice for us now.

Hear Mary Magdalene and those closest to her speak as never before about their human and spiritual lives, and benefit from their energies, experiences, and wisdom to awaken your own Divinely Human nature.

The Third Mary: 55 Messages for Empowering Truth, Peace & Grace from the Mother of Mary Magdalene - The voice of a spiritual adept working silently behind the scenes for eons to help us achieve our greater good is heard here as never before. *The Third Mary's* visionary yet down-to-earth messages are presented verbatim, filled with visions, memories, parables, and advice, as received by channel Roslyn Elena McGrath.

Discover how the mother of a ground-breaking woman and spiritual teacher beyond time can help you to live your Divine humanness more fully and offer your best to our planetary evolution.

Goddess Heart Dancing: A Self Guided Pathway to Light through Imagery, Insights & Inspiration - Bring your wholeness to light by connecting with myriad aspects of the Sacred Feminine within yourself and the Universe. Stunning original art, inspiring messages and poetry, transformative meditdations, and eye-opening self-reflection exercises combine to expand upon the journey begun in *Goddes Heart Rising*, helping you to embody your uniquely sacred self more fully. *Card set also available.*

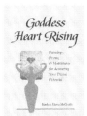

Goddess Heart Rising: Paintings, Poems & Meditations for Activating Your Divine Potential - Benefit from the Goddess energy within and without in new ways with Volume I of the *Goddess Wisdom* series. *Goddess Heart Rising's* messages and imagery guide you in drawing upon your inner resources for greater adventurousness, compassion, self-love, peace, faith, vitality, abundance, fortitude, adaptability, inspiration, assertiveness, and wisdom.

This unique, multi-level journey, born out of the author/artist's ten-year process, will inspire and support you in creating a more empowered, fulfilling life. *Card set also available.*

A New Radiance: Chakra Blessings from the Divine Feminine - Experience five of the Goddesses included in *Goddess Heart Rising*—Kuan Yin, Isis, Lakshmi, Kali, and Ngoshkwe/Star Woman—as living presences and activate their attributes in your body, mind, and life. Gift yourself a new radiance for self-healing and empowerment with these power-packed 7-10 minute meditations.

Chakras Alive! Exploring & Expanding Your Inner Rainbow - If your 9 main chakras could speak, what might they share about your desires, needs, gifts, and challenges? How might they assist you in creating a more balanced, masterful, and fulfilling life?

Chakras Alive!'s activational artwork, poetry, channeled information, guided meditations, key questions, energetic healing techniques, and suggestions for daily living provide a personal guide for novices and experts alike, with cutting-edge information and clear, step-by-step options for putting your chakras' wisdoms into practice.

Chakras Alive! Meditations for Igniting Your Energy Centers - Meet, activate, and expand your nine main energy centers with the nine guided meditations from *Chakras Alive! Exploring & Expanding Your Inner Rainbow*. Narrated by author Roslyn Elena McGrath, with special acoustic background designed to support your chakra system.

Available at www.EmpoweringLightworks.com

Made in the USA
Columbia, SC
29 September 2021